Hoodoo for the Black Child:

Ancestral Altars

By Goddess Ida Mars

Dedicated to my daughter,
Aaliyah, and my future
descendants. Please put some
sweet tea on my altar, too.

I still think of you,

From the time that I
braid and brush my hair

To when I make my
bed. I still think of you.

I miss you. I miss the
times filled with your
laughter

Even when remembering the times you had to be stern with me, I still miss you.

Even though you aren't
physically here with us
anymore, I know you
aren't far away.

Even though you're with Aunt,
Uncle, and the other
ancestors, I know I can still
talk to you when I need to.

Until we meet again, I'll set
up this altar to give us a
space to connect and pray.

Until we meet again, I'll lay
this white cloth down to
represent purity and the sky.

In the corner, I'll place a cool
and clear glass of water for
clarity and flow.

This white candle will
represent fire and purity. It
lights the path of
connection between you
and I.

I'll make sure to get some flowers
in your favorite colors. These
represent remaining grounded and
the earth element.

Until we meet again, I'll light this incense to represent air and flow.

I remember how you liked your coffee,
favorite foods, and sweets. I
remember enjoying them with you.

In remembrance of you, I'll set up this
photo of you.

Here at this altar, I honor and connect with you and all the ancestors that came before. Here, I can ask for help when needed and give thanks.

I still remember the prayer you taught me. You're have always covered me and carried me through.

Ancestral Prayer

I offer these offerings
to all known and unknown ancestors.
To the ancestors who walk with me
to guide me,
To the ancestors who walk before me
to give me sight and clarity,
and to those who walk behind me
to have my back and protect me.
Thank you for doing so and
I ask and am grateful that you continue
to do so.
I pray that with these offerings, you are
blessed.

Come up with your own ancestral pray:

If your grandmother or mom has pictures of loved ones, obituaries, or flowers around her dresser, that is an altar.

"Pouring one out for the homies" is a form of ancestral veneration with origins from ancient Africa.

In Mexican culture, on the Day of the Dead, ancestral altars, or ofrendas, are dedicated to loved ones who have passed.

In some Japanese households, there can be a _butsudan_ or a Buddhist family altar.

Though it might be denied, Christians have ancestral alters for figures such as Jesus, Mary, and the Saints. Could you peep the candles and flowers?

There are many ways we can
remember and honor our loved ones.
How do you celebrate and honor your
loved ones and ancestors?

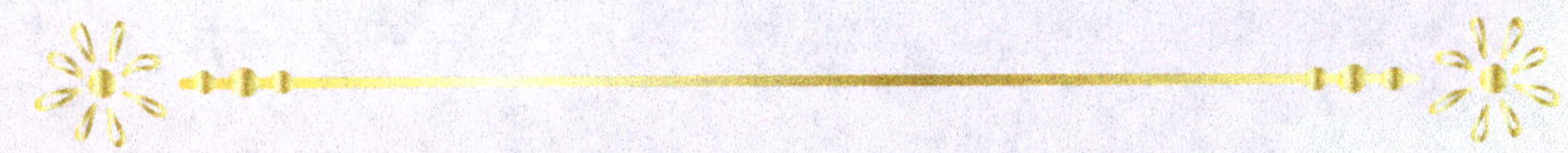

Use the following pages to write the
names of loved ones who have passed,
and draw and write your favorite
memories of them.

This book is only to be used as a guide and not the end all be all. Though some specific traditions and practices exist, create your altar according to how you feel your ancestors led you.